MEDIA CENTER
MARLEY ELEMENTARY SCHOOL

MEDIA CENTER
MARLEY ELEMENTARY SCHOOL

THE WORLD
IN THE TIME OF
ABRAHAM LINCOLN

MEDIA CENTER
MARLEY ELEMENTARY SCHOOL

Chelsea House Publishers
Philadelphia

FIONA MACDONALD

First published in hardback edition in 2001
by Chelsea House Publishers, a subsidiary of
Haights Cross Communications. All rights reserved.
Printed and bound in China.

First published in the UK in 1997 by
Belitha Press Limited, London House,
Great Eastern Wharf, Parkgate Road,
London SW11 4NQ, England

Text copyright © Belitha Press 1997
Text by Fiona Macdonald
Map by Robin Carter, Wildlife Art Agency

Series Editor: Claire Edwards
Editor: Honor Head
Art Director: Helen James
Design: Jamie Asher
Picture Researcher: Diana Morris
Consultant: Sallie Purkiss

First printing
1 3 5 7 9 8 6 4 2

The Chelsea House World Wide Web
address is: **http://www.chelseahouse.com**

Library of Congress Cataloging-in-Publication Data applied for.

ISBN: 0-7910-6028-4

Picture acknowledgements:
AKG, London: 10cr, 16, 39t.
Arcaid: 31c Lucinda Lambton.
Bridgeman Art Library: front cover c British Museum; front cover r N.P.G.
Smithsonian Institution; back cover Victoria & Albert Museum, London;
1c US Embassy, London; 1cr British Library; 4 Private Collection; 7t US
Embassy, London; 10cl Victoria & Albert Museum, London; 10b National
Library of Australia, Canberra; 17cl British Library, London; 17cr National
Library of Australia, Canberra; 18 Private Collection; 22 Victoria & Albert
Museum, London; 23c Royal Geographical Society, London; 24 Baltimore
Museum of Art, Maryland; 25t Private Collection; 29 Royal Geographical
Society, London; 37c American Museum, Bath; 38 British Museum, London;
45 National Library of Australia, Canberra.
British Library, India Office Collection: 27.
Trustees of the British Museum: 16b.
Corbis-Bettmann: cover drop-in, 5b, 11c, 35t, 36, 44b.
E.T. Archive: front cover l Oriental Art Museum, Genoa; 10t, 13b Musée
Malmaison; 15c; 19t National Museum of History, Lima; 21b Historical
Museum, Moscow; 28t Oriental Art Museum, Genoa; 32 Greater London
Record Office; 43 Victoria & Albert Museum, London; 44t Bibliothèque
Nationale, Paris.
Mary Evans Picture Library: 7b, 20b, 26b, 33t, 34, 35c, 37b, 42t.
Hulton Getty Collection: 25b, 42b.

Picture acknowledgements cont:
Frank Lane Picture Agency: 33b.
Mansell Collection: 21t, 23bl.
Peter Newark's Pictures: 1cl, 5t, 6b, 11t, 12, 14b, 20t, 26t, 28b, 30, 31b, 41.
North Wind Picture Archives: 11b, 13t, 15t, 19b, 39b.
Zefa: 3, 40 Damm.

CONTENTS

ABOUT THIS BOOK

This book tells the story of Abraham Lincoln and looks at what was happening all around the world in his time. To help you find your way through the book, each chapter has been divided into seven sections. Each section describes a different part of the world and is headed by a color bar. As you look through a chapter, the color bars tell you which areas you can read about in the text below. There is a time line, to give you an outline of world events in Abraham Lincoln's time, and also a map, which shows some of the most important places mentioned in this book.

On page 46 there is a list of some of the peoples you will read about in this book. Some of the more unfamiliar words are also listed in the glossary.

THE STORY OF ABRAHAM LINCOLN

Abraham Lincoln was the sixteenth President of the United States and one of its greatest leaders. During his lifetime many changes took place in the United States and around the world. In this book you can read about some of these changes. You can also read about how important Abraham Lincoln was in the history of his country. Lincoln lived from 1809 to 1865, but this book covers the time period from 1800 to 1875. This will help you to discover events and ideas that influenced Abraham Lincoln and what happened in the years after he died.

◄This poster shows Lincoln at the time he became president. Above him is the White House in Washington, D.C., which is the official home of the president.

◄Abraham Lincoln was born in this tiny, one-room cabin. It had no glass in the windows and a damp earth floor.

A POOR BEGINNING

Abraham Lincoln was the second child of Thomas Lincoln, and his wife, Nancy Hanks. They lived in wild countryside, known as the "backwoods," in Kentucky, in the southeastern part of the United States. This was a harsh place to live. The weather was warm and humid in summer, but could be very cold in winter. Pioneer farmers who settled in the backwoods had to cut down thick forests and tangled shrubs before they could build their cabins to live in and plant crops.

A NEW MOTHER

Abraham's mother died when he was 9 years old. The following year, his father remarried. Abraham's stepmother, Sarah Johnston, realized that Abraham was a highly intelligent, thoughtful child, and she saw to it that he went to school. Abraham was tall and strong for his age, and his father thought this made him suitable for a life of farm work. But Sarah was convinced that Abraham had a great future ahead of him. She begged his father to give him time off from farmwork so that he could read books and study.

LEAVING THE FARM

When he was 22, Lincoln left the farm and moved to the neighboring state of Illinois where he did all kinds of jobs, including store manager, postmaster, assistant surveyor, and log splitter. In 1837, after teaching himself at home, he qualified as a lawyer. Lincoln became interested in politics and from 1847 to 1849 was a member of Congress. However, because he disapproved of some government policies he became unpopular and was not reelected.

►The law offices in Springfield, Illinois, where Lincoln worked at the time he was elected president

A DIVIDED LAND

In 1783 the United States of America won its independence from Great Britain. For a while the new nation was united in its joy at being free. But by around 1840, the start of Lincoln's political career, there were many disagreements between different states. The most important difference concerned slavery. In the North, slavery was illegal, but it was still legal and very popular in the South. Also, the northern states thought the president should have the power to say how all the states should be run. The southern states wanted him to have less power over them and wanted to run their own state governments by themselves.

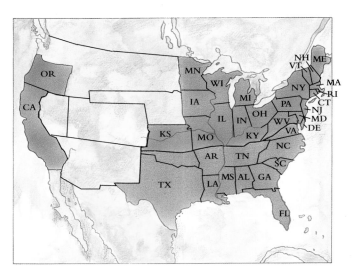

▲ The American Civil War was fought between the states of the Union (blue) that wanted to abolish slavery and the states of the Confederacy (red) that wanted to keep slavery. The yellow area was ruled by the US government but had not yet been organized into separate states.

FIGHT AGAINST SLAVERY

Abraham Lincoln was born in a southern state, where slavery was legal, but spent most of his adult life in Illinois, where slavery was banned. In 1854, Congress, supported by the southern states, passed an act allowing the settlers in the new frontier territories to decide whether they wanted slavery. Lincoln believed that slavery was evil. He felt that it was very bad to have states where slavery was allowed, and he wanted slavery to be banned throughout the nation. In 1856 he joined the newly formed Republican Party and promised to fight against the spread of slavery.

◄ Sugar plantations in the southern states were worked by slaves. Originally slaves were shipped to America from Africa, but by Abraham Lincoln's time many had been born to slave parents already living in the United States. Slaves were often cruelly treated by their owners and had no civil rights.

◀This statue of President Lincoln was made almost 100 years after he died. Today Lincoln is remembered for his fight against slavery and his belief in democracy.

CIVIL WAR

Lincoln was elected president in 1860. But soon there was trouble. The following year, 11 southern states broke away from the rest to form their own government. They did not want President Lincoln to ban slavery in their lands. Civil war broke out as southerners attacked northerners.

THE END OF SLAVERY

In 1863, Lincoln issued the Emancipation Proclamation, making slavery illegal. He was elected president for a second term in 1864. By that time the southern states were growing weak. Without slaves to work on their farms, landowners were becoming poor, and southern troops were short of food and weapons. But in the north, farmers, factories, shipbuilders, gun foundries, and the people who worked there prospered.

A NATIONAL HERO

The Civil War finally ended on April 9, 1865. Thanks to Lincoln's leadership and the skills of brilliant army generals, the northern states won. Slavery was abolished throughout the United States, and all the states were still governed by one president. Lincoln was a hero. But Lincoln did not have much time to enjoy his achievements. On April 14, 1865, he was shot and badly wounded. He died the next day.

▶Abraham Lincoln was shot while he was watching a play at a Washington theater. His attacker was a promising actor named John Wilkes Booth, who supported the southern states.

THE WORLD 1800-1875

ABOUT THE MAPS

The maps on this page will help you find your way around. The big map shows some of the places mentioned in the text, including:

- **COUNTRIES,** including some that are different from those today.
- *Past peoples,* such as the Mandan. The descendants of these peoples often live in the same place today, but their traditional lifestyles have almost vanished.
- *GEOGRAPHICAL FEATURES,* including mountains and rivers.
- *Towns and cities.* To find the position of a town or city, look for the name in the list below and then find the number on the map.

1	Salt Lake City	7	Istanbul
2	Washington	8	Aden
3	New Orleans	9	Bombay
4	Charleston	10	Calcutta
5	New York	11	Canton (Guangzhou)
6	Manchester	12	Singapore

The little map shows the world divided into seven regions. The people who lived in a region were linked by customs, traditions, beliefs, or simply by their environment. There were many differences within each region, but the people living there had more in common with one another than with people elsewhere. Each region is shown in a different color—the same colors are used in the headings throughout the book.

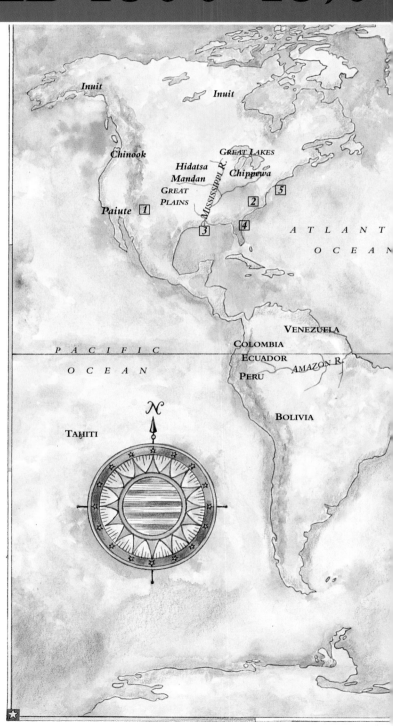

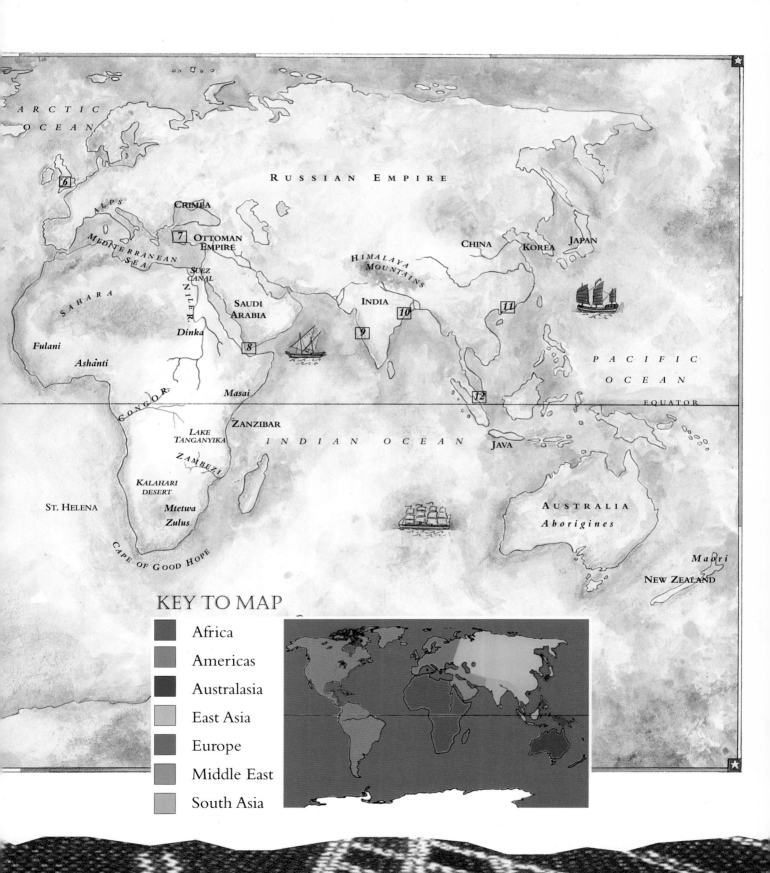

ARCTIC OCEAN

RUSSIAN EMPIRE

6

ALPS

CRIMEA

MEDITERRANEAN SEA

7   OTTOMAN EMPIRE

SUEZ CANAL

SAHARA

NILE R.

Dinka

SAUDI ARABIA

HIMALAYA MOUNTAINS

INDIA

CHINA   KOREA   JAPAN

Fulani

Ashanti

8

9

10

11

PACIFIC OCEAN

CONGO R.

Masai

12

EQUATOR

ZANZIBAR

LAKE TANGANYIKA

ZAMBEZI

INDIAN OCEAN

JAVA

KALAHARI DESERT

ST. HELENA

Mtetwa

Zulus

AUSTRALIA
Aborigines

CAPE OF GOOD HOPE

Maori

NEW ZEALAND

KEY TO MAP

- Africa
- Americas
- Australasia
- East Asia
- Europe
- Middle East
- South Asia

TIME LINE

1800

AMERICAS

1803 United States buys Louisiana Territory from France and doubles in size.

1808–1828 Revolts in South America; Spanish colonies win independence.

1808 U.S. bans import of slaves from Africa.

1811 Shawnee leader Tecumseh leads Native Americans in fighting settlers on their land. Native Americans defeated at the Battle of Tippecanoe.

1818 Borders agreed between U.S. and Canada.

1812–1815 War between Britain and U.S.

1828 Work begun first railroad in U.S. between Baltimore and Ohio.

EUROPE

1804 Napoleon becomes Emperor of France.

1805 Battle of Trafalgar.

1815 Battle of Waterloo.

1821 In Britain, Faraday invents the electric motor.

1822 In France, Niepce invents photography.

1825 In Britain, first passenger railway from Stockton to Darlington.

MIDDLE EAST

1804 Serbs revolt against Ottoman rule.

1811 Wahhabi Saudi dynasty controls most of Arabia.

1821 Greeks revolt against Ottoman rule.

SOUTH ASIA

1815 First Gurkha regiment recruited in Nepal.

1815 British occupy Ceylon (present-day Sri Lanka).

1819 Singapore founded as a free trade port.

1825–1830 Javanese people revolt against Dutch colonial rulers.

EAST ASIA

1800 Britain begins importing opium into China.

1802 Siam (present-day Thailand) conquers Cambodia.

AFRICA

1806 British take control of Cape Colony, South Africa.

1807 Slave trade abolished throughout British Empire.

1811 Muhammad Ali takes control of Egypt.

1816 Shaka Zulu founds kingdom in South Africa.

1822 Muhammad Ali conquers Sudan.

1822 Liberia founded as a colony for freed slaves.

1824 Ashante people of present-day Ghana fight against British would-be colonizers.

AUSTRALASIA

1803 First circumnavigation of Australia.

1803 New British convict colony founded in Tasmania.

1810 Hawaiian Islands united.

1814 First European missionaries arrive in New Zealand.

1825 Maori in New Zealand drive away would-be European settlers.

1875

1833 The *New York Sun*, first cheap daily paper launched.

1859 First oil well drilled in Pennsylvania.

1860s Apache leader Geronimo leads fight against European settlers.

1874 First electric streetcar in New York.
1875 Telephone invented by Alexander Graham Bell.

1841 First college degrees awarded to American women.

1837 Morse Code invented by William Morse.

1833 In Britain, first laws to protect factory workers.

1859 Garibaldi begins war to unite Italy.

1858 In France, Pasteur discovers that bacteria cause disease.

1861 Russian serfs freed.

1845 Famine in Ireland.

1840 First postage stamp in Britain.

1863 First underground railway in London.

1839 Britain takes control of Aden, an important trading port on the Red Sea.

1860 Revolution against Ottomans in Syria.

1860 Civil war in Lebanon.

1869 Suez Canal opens.

1853–1856 Crimean War.

1861 Bahrain becomes a British protectorate.

1853 First railroads and telegraph in India.

1857 Indian Mutiny.

1843–1849 Britain conquers Sind, Punjab, and Kashmir, parts of present-day India and Pakistan.

1842 Britain takes control of Hong Kong.

1854 First treaty between Japan and U.S.

1863 France takes control of Cambodia.

1856–1860 Second Opium War.

1839–1842 First Opium War between China and Britain.

1850–1864 Taiping Rebellion by Chinese against weak Chinese Emperor.

1868 Meiji dynasty comes to power in Japan and begins program of industrialization.

1830 France begins to conquer Algeria.

1853 Livingstone begins famous journey to western Africa.

1867 Diamonds discovered in South Africa.

1835 Boers begin Great Trek northward from southern Africa.

1840 Treaty of Waitangi – Britain takes control of New Zealand.

1851 Australian gold rush.

1860 Maori Wars between Maori and settlers in New Zealand.

1844 New South Wales, one of the Australian states, refuses to take any more British convicts.

1861 Gold discovered in New Zealand.

AROUND THE WORLD

During Abraham Lincoln's life three major changes were happening around the world. First, families from all over Europe left their homelands to settle in new countries, especially in the United States, as Lincoln's ancestors had done. Second, Lincoln was interested in new forms of government that would improve people's civil rights, and there were demands for similar reforms in many other countries. Third, toward the end of his life, Lincoln led his country through a savage civil war. Riots and revolutions were also happening in many other lands.

▲ Fighting in the American Civil War. This painting shows northern troops capturing the southern city of Petersburg, Virginia, in April 1865.

▲ Pioneers traveling across the United States faced many dangers. They had to cross wide rivers, high, rocky mountains, and scorching deserts.

THE U.S. GROWS

AMERICAS

The United States was still a very new country when Abraham Lincoln was born. It was created in 1776 when 13 colonies broke away from British rule and declared themselves independent. The United States of America grew rapidly as more states joined the Union. Some were purchased, some were conquered, and some were acquired in peace treaties. Others, mostly to the west of the Mississippi River, were simply taken over by pioneer farmers. These new states were not empty. Native Americans had lived there for thousands of years. As settlers moved westward, taking land from the Native Americans, there were many quarrels and fights.

NAPOLEON AT WAR

EUROPE

The early years of Abraham Lincoln's life saw dramatic events in Europe such as invasions, new governments, and some of the bloodiest battles ever fought on land or sea. Much of this was caused by one person, Napoleon Bonaparte. Napoleon first won fame as a brave young soldier in the French Revolution, which began in 1789. He led armies throughout Europe, inspired by the ideas of "liberty" and "equality." But soon he wanted power just for himself. In 1799 he seized control of the French government. In 1804 he crowned himself Emperor of France and set out to conquer as many lands as he could. At first he won many victories. He toppled many European governments and set up his own men in their place. But when he tried to invade Russia in 1812, his army ran out of food and had to retreat. Over half a million soldiers died, trapped in the Russian winter snows.

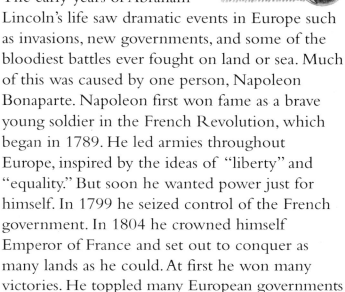

► This detail is from a painting that shows Napoleon giving orders to his soldiers as they march across the Alps to conquer Italy. As a ruler of France, Napoleon introduced many reforms in laws, education, and government that still influence French life today.

THE FUTURE FOR EUROPE

EUROPE

In 1815 an army from several European countries, led by Britain's Duke of Wellington, defeated the French at the Battle of Waterloo. Napoleon was forced into exile on the remote island of Saint Helena in the South Atlantic Ocean, where he died in 1821.

While Napeoleon was in exile, an international meeting was held in Vienna, Austria, to decide how Europe should be governed in the future. Many kings and politicians whom Napoleon had dismissed were restored to power. But new ideas from the French Revolution and from Napoleon's reforms in France had already spread to many countries in Europe, South America, and the Middle East.

FREEDOM FROM SERFDOM

As much as half the Russian population, about 20 million people, were serfs. This meant that they belonged to their landlord. They had to work hard for him without any pay and were not allowed to leave his lands. If they refused to obey orders, they could be cruelly punished or even killed. In many ways their lives were as terrible as those of American slaves.

Throughout the nineteenth century, Russian serfs demanded freedom, but serfdom was not abolished until 1861. After Russia's defeat in the Crimean War, Alexander II became very unpopular. He feared a massive uprising if he did not agree to the serfs' demands. But even after they were freed from serfdom, many Russian people were still very poor.

PEOPLE POWER

The Ottoman Empire was based in the city of Constantinople (Istanbul) in Turkey. It was the most powerful state in the Middle East. But in the nineteenth century, it was threatened by nationalism, the wish of conquered people to rule themselves. A revolt against the Ottomans started in Greece in 1821.

▶ A well-armed Greek freedom fighter. A nationalist revolt against the Ottoman Empire started in Greece. Volunteers from Britain, France, and Russia helped the Greek people to fight. Greece finally won independence in 1832.

EMPIRE UNDER THREAT

The Ottoman Empire was also threatened by Russia, which had captured many Ottoman lands around the Black Sea. Russian rulers wanted access to warm-water Black Sea ports, since their own harbors were blocked by ice in winter. Britain and France were also worried because they feared Russia would soon control all Asia, including trade routes to the rich land of India. From 1853 to 1856, Britain and France fought and won a war against Russia in the Crimea and captured the Russian port of Sevastopol.

◀ The Charge of the Light Brigade took place during the Battle of Balaklava (1854) at the beginning of the Crimean War. Six hundred British soldiers on horseback and armed only with sabers misunderstood their orders. They charged toward the Russians, who were armed with heavy guns. About 40 percent were killed.

THE EAST INDIA COMPANY

Since the early sixteenth century, India had been ruled by emperors from the Mogul dynasty, but by Abraham Lincoln's time they were weak and had lost control. Parts of India were ruled by Indian warrior princes, but many of the strongest, richest rulers were not Indian at all. They were a group of British merchants, working for an international trading organization called the East India Company. It had its own private army, made laws, collected taxes, and controlled India's trade.

▲ The city of Calcutta, in India, was founded by East India Company merchants in 1690. This view was painted in 1815.

THE INDIAN MUTINY

In 1857, Indian troops in the East India Company's army mutinied. They attacked British officers and civilians and captured many important towns. The mutiny lasted for almost a year. As a result, in 1858 the British government took control. It decided that in the future India was to be ruled from London. The East India Company had its powers reduced. The last Mogul emperor was dismissed and replaced by Queen Victoria.

◀British drug dealers encouraged Chinese people to develop the dangerous habit of smoking opium by helping Chinese traders smuggle opium into China. This drawing, made around 1850, shows smugglers lowering bales of opium over a city wall.

OPIUM WARS

EAST ASIA

Chinese rulers had been so proud of their economic success and of their ancient civilization that they refused to have any contact with the West. But Britain and other European states were eager to trade with China. They realized they could make huge sums of money through trade, especially by selling opium to the Chinese. This soon led to wars between 1839 and 1842 and 1856 and 1860. China was defeated and was forced to give European merchants the right to travel and trade throughout China.

LAND OF MANY CULTURES

AFRICA

The continent of Africa was divided into many different countries. Large areas of West Africa were governed by the Fulani dynasty, who ruled their rich kingdoms according to Muslim law. West African kingdoms, like the Ashanti of Ghana, had also grown rich through crafts and trade. In East Africa, the Kabakas of Buganda ruled a splendid empire in present-day Uganda and nearby lands.

►Bronze head made in the West African kingdom of Benin. It shows a nineteenth-century ruler wearing a splendid crown.

ZULUS AND BOERS

There were troubles between British and Dutch settlers in South Africa. The British governor tried to keep the Dutch settlers, called Boers, from mistreating their African workers. But the Boers refused to obey British laws. Between 1835 and 1840, about 12,000 Boer farmers left their homes at the southern tip of Africa and trekked northward through wild and dangerous countryside in search of new land where they could live free from British rule. Along the way, many Boers were killed by Zulu warriors when they trespassed on Zulu land.

▼ Boer farmers and their families traveled in wagons pulled by oxen.

DISCOVERING THE SOUTH PACIFIC

AUSTRALASIA

After Captain James Cook's voyages from 1768 to 1779, European nations became aware of the vast size and richness of the South Pacific lands. They saw them as empty territory to be taken and used. They did not consider the rights of the Aborigines and Maori who lived there.

CONVICT SETTLEMENTS

The first Europeans to settle in Australia were the British convicts, transported there in 1788 as punishment for their crimes. Then, in 1793, the first free settlers arrived, hoping to set up ranches and farms. Eventually, released convicts also built homes in Australia and New Zealand.

▲ Chief Palou entertaining sailors from the French ship *Astrolabe* on the Pacific island of Tonga. At first, European sailors were welcomed by Pacific peoples. This friendship turned to war when European settlers started to seize their land.

WHALERS AND HUNTERS

European whalers, hunters, and traders came to settle in New Zealand, and European farmers imported vast flocks of sheep to New Zealand. Between 1843 and 1872, settlers clashed with local Maori farmers in a series of fierce battles known as the Maori Wars. In a similar way French sailors and settlers took over many Pacific islands by force. They occupied the beautiful and very useful deep-water harbor at Tahiti in 1842.

FAMOUS RULERS AND LEADERS

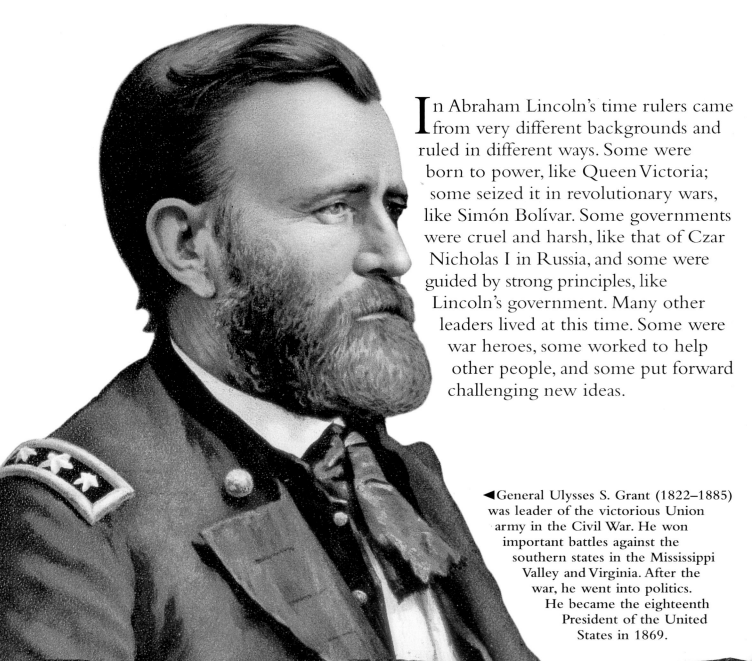

In Abraham Lincoln's time rulers came from very different backgrounds and ruled in different ways. Some were born to power, like Queen Victoria; some seized it in revolutionary wars, like Simón Bolívar. Some governments were cruel and harsh, like that of Czar Nicholas I in Russia, and some were guided by strong principles, like Lincoln's government. Many other leaders lived at this time. Some were war heroes, some worked to help other people, and some put forward challenging new ideas.

◀General Ulysses S. Grant (1822–1885) was leader of the victorious Union army in the Civil War. He won important battles against the southern states in the Mississippi Valley and Virginia. After the war, he went into politics. He became the eighteenth President of the United States in 1869.

THE GREAT ESCAPE

AMERICAS

Abraham Lincoln was only one of many people who campaigned against slavery in America. Harriet Tubman (c. 1820–1913), an escaped slave, lived in the state of Maryland. Together with friends, Tubman set up a network of secret trackways and overnight hiding places called "the Underground Railroad." It was used by thousands of slaves who had run away from their owners and were trying to reach Canada or the northern states where slavery had been banned. This was a dangerous operation. If Tubman had been caught, she would have been severely punished, or even killed. When the Civil War broke out in 1861, Tubman used her experience to undertake secret missions for Abraham Lincoln's army, as a scout and a spy.

►Historians estimate that Harriet Tubman personally helped hundreds of slaves to escape to freedom between 1850 and 1860.

▲ Simón Bolívar, the South American revolutionary leader

FOREIGN RULE

Ever since the sixteenth century, large parts of South America had been ruled by European nations. In the early nineteenth century, many South American colonies rebelled and declared themselves independent from European colonial rule. Simón Bolívar (1783–1830), called "the Liberator," was the greatest South American revolutionary leader. He managed to help no less than five countries fight to win their freedom. He is still considered the "founding father" of Venezuela, Colombia, Ecuador, Peru, and Bolivia—which was named after him.

ADMIRAL NELSON

EUROPE

The top two British commanders who fought against Napoleon are still remembered as heroes in Britain. Admiral Horatio Lord Nelson (1758–1805) came from a poor clergyman's family and joined the Navy when he was only 12 years old. After many early successes in battle, where he lost his right eye and his right arm, he was chosen to command the British fleet against the French and Spanish at Trafalgar, off the coast of Spain, in 1805. He won the battle but was wounded. He died on board his ship, the H.M.S. *Victory*.

DUKE OF WELLINGTON

Arthur Wellesley, Duke of Wellington (1769–1852), also proved his skill when still a young man. In 1796 he was sent to India, to fight Indian princes who were rebelling against the British. He won a victory for Britain. Back in Europe, Wellington led British soldiers against Napoleon's troops when they invaded Portugal and Spain and beat Napoleon at the battle of Waterloo in 1815. In 1820, Wellington went into politics.

► Admiral Lord Nelson was a bold, unconventional character who was highly respected and liked by his sailors. They told many stories about his adventures, like the time he put his telescope to his blind eye to avoid seeing a signal sent by his commanding officer that he did not want to obey.

▲ Victoria and Albert married in 1840 and had nine children. Prince Albert worked hard to encourage the latest developments in science and technology.

QUEEN VICTORIA

It was unusual for a woman to be head of state in Abraham Lincoln's time. Yet Princess Victoria (1819–1901) was an only child and was brought up knowing that one day she would be queen. She was given a careful education to prepare her for her future duties and was crowned in 1837 when she was only 18 years old. She is the longest-reigning monarch in British history. Victoria married in 1840 and had nine children. Throughout her life she took a keen interest in politics and foreign affairs. Sometimes she disagreed with government policies, but she tried not to interfere. At times, Victoria was not a very popular ruler. People felt she was too distant and aloof and not in touch with the lives of ordinary people. But by the end of her long reign, she was loved and respected as the head of one of the richest and most powerful nations in the world.

OTTOMAN REFORMS

MIDDLE EAST

In Abraham Lincoln's time, much of the Middle East was ruled by sultans from the Ottoman dynasty, which had been in power since around 1300. Sultan Selim III (reigned 1789–1807) tried to modernize the old-style Ottoman army and government. He planned a series of changes to the tax laws and the system of land ownership. But he faced fierce opposition from traditionalists at home. Selim was forced to resign and was then murdered by his political enemies.

▼Czar Nicholas I began the Crimean War by attacking the Ottoman Empire. He died before the Crimean War ended, and his son took over.

▶Ottoman sultan Abdul-Medjid tried to reform the ancient Ottoman Empire and stop its slow decline.

SUPERPOWERS

Later Ottoman sultans, like Abdul-Medjid I (ruled 1839–1861), had more success with reforms. Abdul-Medjid reorganized the royal court and the education system, and gave citizens better civil rights. To protect the northern part of his empire from Russian attack, he made alliances with Britain and France. Elsewhere, rulers and leaders had very different ambitions. In Afghanistan, Jamal al-Din al Afghani (1838-1897) campaigned for a union of all Islamic nations. He wanted to create a Muslim superstate. In contrast, Czar Nicholas I of Russia (ruled 1825-1855) wanted to create a mighty Russian Empire with himself as its leader. He crushed all calls for freedom and democracy, and tried to conquer new lands by attacking Ottoman territory.

FIGHTING EUROPEAN RULE

Many of South Asia's leaders spent their lives fighting against European rule. On the rich coffee-growing island of Java, Indonesia, Prince Dipanegara (1785–1855) led a revolt against the Dutch colonists who had taken control of his kingdom. But his bold plans ended in tragedy. In the war that followed his revolt, between 1825 and 1830, over 200,000 Javanese people were killed, and Dipanegara was exiled.

INDIAN INDEPENDENCE

In India, Tipu Sultan, ruler of Mysore, and Laksmibai, Rani of Jhansi, both fought bravely against the British, who wanted to take over their lands. Tipu died in the last desperate, unsuccessful battle to save his kingdom in 1799. When British troops captured Jhansi in 1857, Laksmibai escaped and went to join other Indian princes fighting against British rule. She was one of the bravest fighters in the battle, and people at the time said she was one of the best army commanders they had ever seen. She died from wounds received in battle in 1858.

REVOLUTION IN JAPAN

In 1868, after a short civil war, a new style of government came to power in Japan. For centuries shoguns (army generals) had run the country on behalf of the emperor. Now new political leaders took the place of the shoguns. They were well-educated men, mostly from noble families, who had worked as government officials but were eager for change.

LEARNING FROM THE WORLD

Leading members of Japanese society included Kido Koin and Iwasaki Yataro. They introduced new laws, a new constitution, and new policies designed to modernize the economy and society. They encouraged foreign experts to come to Japan and went on study trips abroad. Some of these leaders, like Yataro, founded successful businesses. In 1873, he set up the Mitsubishi trading company. It dealt in banking, insurance, mining, and shipping. By 1877, Mitsubishi owned 80 percent of all ships in Japan.

▼ Tipu Sultan (his name meant Tiger King) kept this lifesize model of a tiger devouring a European officer in his palace. A mechanism inside the tiger made a roaring noise.

SHAKA, KING OF THE ZULUS

In South Africa the powerful figure of Shaka, king of the Zulu people from 1816 to 1828, played a leading part in events. The Zulus were just one small clan belonging to a much larger African nation, the Mtetwa. But Shaka wanted his people to be independent. He developed a deadly new way of fighting, using a short, stabbing spear called an assegai. Zulu warriors soon overpowered the Mtetwa nation and Shaka became king. Shaka's next plan was to win more land. The Zulus conquered vast territories in southeast Africa, forcing the African peoples who lived there to run for their lives. So many people were forced to flee that Shaka's reign became known as "Mfecane"—"time of troubles."

▲ King Shaka became a hero to many Zulu people in South Africa. This drawing shows him negotiating a treaty with English army officers.

SETTLERS AND CHIEFS

In Australia and New Zealand, leaders and chiefs faced the problem of how they could stop well-armed European settlers from taking over their lands. In Australia, governors sent by Britain tried to bring peace by teaching the Aborigines European customs or by transporting them away from the settlers' land. In New Zealand, quarrels between local chiefs and settlers led to fights, raids, and eventually to war.

▲ Maori warriors performing a war dance in front of a statue of a god.

TREATY OF WAITANGI

In 1840 the British government persuaded Maori chiefs to sign the Treaty of Waitangi. This said that the British would protect the Maori lands if the Maori allowed settlers to come and live peacefully in New Zealand and let the British government rule. Thousands of British settlers flocked to New Zealand, ignored the treaty, and settled on Maori land. The British government refused to help the Maori get their land back, so in 1843 and in 1860, the Maori declared war. Peace was finally made in 1881.

HOW PEOPLE LIVED

The world in Abraham Lincoln's time was full of contrasts, especially in the way people lived. In some areas, such as parts of Asia, people followed lifestyles that had changed very little in thousands of years. In other regions, such as Western Europe, new inventions meant that the lives of ordinary people were changing at a dizzying pace. In Australia, Africa, and parts of the United States, native peoples with lifestyles handed down over generations, came face to face with new settlers who had completely different customs and ideas. In most instances the old, traditional lifestyles were destroyed by the settlers.

▲ This painting dated 1834 shows the inside of an earth lodge house. It was built by Mandan Native Americans, who lived in present-day North Dakota.

NATIVE AMERICAN LIVES

AMERICAS

Throughout North and South America and the Caribbean, several different lifestyles existed side by side. The oldest belonged to the hundreds of Native American groups who lived in very different environments, from high mountains to scorching deserts. The Inuit people of the Arctic hunted seals and walrus, while along the northwest coast the Chinook trapped salmon and speared whales.

On the Great Plains the Mandan and Hidatsa hunted herds of buffalo and planted fields of corn and beans. In the western deserts, the Paiute gathered grubs, seeds, and nuts. In South American rain forests, native peoples ate roots and fruit and hunted snakes and monkeys. Farmers in the high Andes Mountains raised herds of llamas for milk, meat, and wool.

▼ A busy street in New Orleans in 1862, crowded with horse-drawn carriages and trams

▲ Miners went to California hoping to get rich by striking gold. They dug up rocky mountain slopes or "panned."

GOLD HUNTERS

Abraham Lincoln's early life (see page 5) was like that of many farmers who moved inland from the earliest European settlements along the eastern coast. When gold was discovered in California in 1848, miners and fortune-hunters joined farmers and their families making the long, dangerous journey overland. Along the way, many died from disease and exhaustion, or after drinking poisonous water from desert springs.

CONTRASTS

In southern cities, such as Charleston and New Orleans, there were elegant houses, hospitals, colleges, theaters, restaurants, and shops. This prosperous lifestyle was, however, based on wealth created by the suffering of slaves, who were forced to work long hours in hot, humid temperatures picking cotton and cutting sugar cane. They lived in shacks on their master's land and could be beaten or even killed if they tried to run away.

CHANGING TIMES

EUROPE

In many parts of Europe, new machines and new ways of working were transforming traditional farming and manufacturing techniques. Historians call these changes the Agricultural Revolution and the Industrial Revolution (see page 31).

THE AGRICULTURAL REVOLUTION

The Agricultural Revolution began around 1700 and continued for almost 150 years. Landowners increased farm production by introducing new crop rotations, drainage, and manuring systems; by breeding stronger cattle; and by enclosing and plowing commons and wasteland. These changes were profitable for landowners but caused problems for ordinary people. Many had no land of their own to grow food for their families, and without public land and wasteland areas, they had nowhere to graze a cow or keep a few sheep. The only regular work was on the landlords' farms, but because the population was increasing, wages were low and food prices high.

▲In Ireland the soil was poor and the climate was cool and wet. Ordinary people survived by growing potatoes to eat. Between 1845 and 1847, the potato crop was destroyed by blight (disease). This caused widespread famine, and thousands of people died. Many of them left Ireland for a better life in the United States.

◀Life in factory towns, which grew as a result of the Industrial Revolution, was miserable. Workers faced long hours, low pay, and terrible accidents. Workers' houses were cold, cramped, and dirty. Both air and water were polluted by smoke and dust from factories, and there were few shops or open spaces or parks. This painting shows a typical industrial area in the Midlands, England, around 1850.

SHIPPING AND SHOPPING

MIDDLE EAST

In many parts of the Middle East, merchants and craft workers lived in noisy, crowded towns. They sold handmade goods, such as carpets, brassware, pottery, leather saddles, and slippers in busy marketplaces called "souks." Ports like Aden, which were on busy shipping routes to India and beyond, grew much bigger and richer after the Suez Canal (see page 35) was opened. They sold fresh food and water for the ships, and souvenirs to the passengers on board.

CASH CROPS

In the countryside, farmers raised flocks of sheep and goats; planted apple, orange, apricot, and almond orchards and olive trees; and raised crops of grains, vegetables, and melons. In Iran, the farmers grew large fields of cash crops such as tobacco for sale to big international companies based in Europe and the United States. When there was a world shortage, prices were high. But if there was too much, prices fell, and sometimes the farmers could not afford to buy food.

CHANGES IN INDIA

SOUTH ASIA

At the beginning of the nineteenth century, many fine goods made by Indian craft workers were exported to Europe. Brightly colored silks and delicate cottons were especially sought-after. The Industrial Revolution in Europe meant that machines in British factories could produce cotton cloth more cheaply than Indian hand-weavers. Now Indian farmers exported raw cotton to England and in return had to buy British factory-made cotton cloth. As a result, many Indian weavers were put out of work.

MANGOES AND COCONUTS

Indian farmers grew a wide variety of crops, from grains in the north to rice, mangoes, and coconuts in the south. Some of these crops fed farmers' families, some were paid as taxes, and some were sold in market towns. Farmers' homes varied, too, from sunbaked mud-brick houses in the deserts of Rajasthan, to wickerwork shelters roofed with palm-leaf thatch in the hot, muddy fields of Bengal.

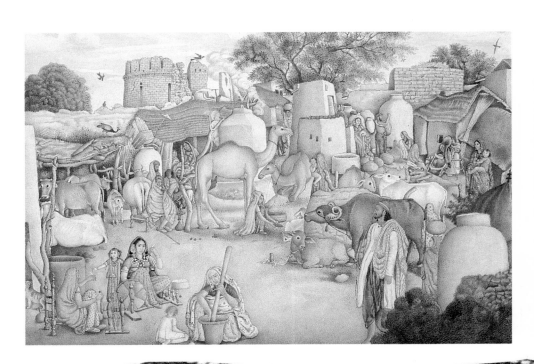

►A village in northwest India, painted around 1800. Many villages were laid out according to the Hindu caste system. This divided people into four religious classes, plus a group of "untouchables," who were believed to be "impure." Top-ranking families lived in the center of the village. Untouchables had to live outside.

GROWING POPULATION

EAST ASIA

By the early nineteenth century, the population of China had increased dramatically. For many people in the countryside, life was a constant struggle to produce enough food to feed themselves and their families. In good years, when the rivers did not flood their fields or when typhoons did not sink their fishing boats, farmers managed to survive. But in bad years many starved. Others left China to work in terrible conditions building railroads in Canada or the United States or digging mines and unloading ships in Malaysia and Singapore.

TREATY PORTS

During the eighteenth century, Chinese rulers kept British merchants out of China because they believed that Chinese goods were better than anything "foreign devils" could supply. But after 1842, Chinese emperors were forced to allow European merchants to set up "treaty ports," like the city of Canton (now Guangzhou). Chinese bankers, builders, traders, craft workers, and shipowners set up thriving businesses there, and British merchants traded with immensely wealthy Chinese businessmen called taipans.

▲ A print by Japanese artist Hiroshige, showing the traditional way of planting rice used in many East Asian lands.

TRADITIONAL LIFESTYLES

AFRICA

In most of Africa traditional lifestyles continued throughout the century. On dry savanna grasslands, peoples such as the Masai (of present-day Kenya) and the Dinka (of present-day Sudan) lived as herders and hunters. In tropical West Africa, people lived in farming communities and grew crops of plantains and yams. Farther south, farmers grew millet and sorghum and raised cattle and goats.

◀ The East African island of Zanzibar (part of present-day Tanzania) continued as a center of slave trade long after slave trading had been abolished in West Africa.

SPLENDID TOWNS

Along the east and west coasts, there were many large and splendid towns. The West African city of Kumasi (in present-day Ghana), capital of the rich, gold-mining Ashanti nation, was famous for its wide streets lined with houses decorated in shiny red and white clay. Underground drains and teams of sweepers made sure the city was kept healthful and clean.

VILLAGES AND FARMS

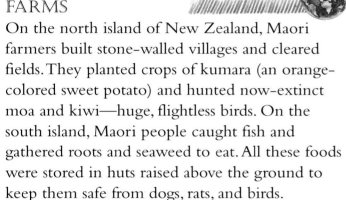

AUSTRALASIA

On the north island of New Zealand, Maori farmers built stone-walled villages and cleared fields. They planted crops of kumara (an orange-colored sweet potato) and hunted now-extinct moa and kiwi—huge, flightless birds. On the south island, Maori people caught fish and gathered roots and seaweed to eat. All these foods were stored in huts raised above the ground to keep them safe from dogs, rats, and birds.

THE ABORIGINE WAY

At the beginning of the nineteenth century, there were probably about 1 million Aborigines living in Australia. They survived in one of the harshest, driest environments in the world by using skills that had been handed down for thousands of years. These included gathering seeds and wild fruits, hunting kangaroos, fishing along the coast, trapping eels in wicker cages and birds in nets, and digging for roots and grubs.

THE NEW SETTLERS ARRIVE

In just one decade, between 1852 and 1861, over 343,000 settlers migrated to Australia from overseas. Most settlers chose to live in Australia because they hoped for a new life and a chance to get rich—either from gold mining or from raising enormous flocks of sheep. Wool and meat from sheep were exported to Europe in large quantities to supply cloth factories and to feed the growing populations.

►Maori village homes were built of wood. Houses like this one, which belonged to a powerful chief, were decorated with magnificent carvings of heroes and gods.

DISCOVERY AND INVENTION

During Abraham Lincoln's lifetime, there were more scientific inventions and discoveries than in any similar period before. They took place in all areas of human knowledge from archaeology to zoology. Steam power replaced wind and water power, and mass production replaced traditional craft skills. All these inventions and discoveries were made in Europe and the United States. They gave the countries that developed them political and economic advantages over the rest of the world.

▲ An American express train, pulled by a coal-fired locomotive, 1864. New forms of transportation, such as railroads and steamships, made it possible to travel much farther and faster than ever before.

A CHANGING WORLD

AMERICAS

In such a vast continent as North America, the development of transportation and communications was especially important. In 1869 one could travel across the United States by train. Telegraph wires ran alongside the tracks to carry messages instantly. Then in 1875 the American Alexander Graham Bell designed the first telephone. People could now talk to one another across thousands of miles. Americans also invented many other things that changed people's lives, such as typewriters, sewing machines, and mechanical harvesters.

FACTORY GOODS

EUROPE

In many European countries newly invented machines in huge factories replaced craft workers who made goods by hand at home. Soon machines were mass-producing cloth, glass, and pottery. Factories also produced cast iron, steel, and cement. New materials and new building technology changed the way bridges, tunnels, and tall buildings were built.

USEFUL MACHINES

Factories also produced machines such as reapers and binders to help with farmwork and steam engines to replace horses. Factories were built in towns with good supplies of water and coal to provide steam power. Millions of men, women, and children moved from the country to industrial towns seeking jobs.

►The "waterfall" toilet, mass-produced in an English pottery factory around 1880. Thomas Crapper designed the first really efficient flush toilet at the end of the nineteenth century.

IMPORTANT RESEARCH

Scientific researchers in nineteenth-century Europe made many important discoveries in biology, physics, chemistry, medicine, and mathematics. Some developments, such as long-lasting fabric dyes, electricity, and extra-strong kinds of steel, were useful for new industries. Some, such as the discovery of antiseptics and anesthetics, improved medical care. Some, like Babbage's "difference engine" (mechanical computer) of 1823 and Niépce's experiments with photography (1827), paved the way for inventions that would be very important in later years.

◄ This picture shows steel plate being made in a factory in the town of Sheffield, England.

NEW WAYS OF WAR

During the nineteenth century new inventions and discoveries changed the way wars were fought. Breech-loading rifles were used in the Crimean War (see pages 14–15) and in the U.S. Civil War. Loaded from the back end of the barrel, they were faster to load and fire than earlier types of guns. The Crimean War was also the first war in which underwater mines fitted with explosives and a detonator (a device to make them go off) were used to sink enemy ships. Wartime events also encouraged scientific research. After the French Black Sea fleet was badly damaged by an unexpected storm, army and navy commanders began to demand more accurate weather forecasting, and scientists in many lands began to keep more detailed records of the weather.

SHOCKING NEWS

For the first time army commanders in the Crimean War used the newly invented electric telegraph to send urgent messages to government leaders. Journalists also telegraphed reports to their newspapers. Readers were shocked when they read these eyewitness accounts of the terrible fighting and saw the first-ever newspaper photos of battle scenes and men injured in war.

▼ More men died during the Crimean War from disease than in battle. When British nurse Florence Nightingale arrived in the Crimea, she was appalled at the conditions she found there. She immediately organized proper hygiene and better nursing care. Later she set up schools where professional nurses could be trained.

◄In areas of South Asia, such as northeast India and Sri Lanka, huge tea plantations were created by European estate owners. Local women picked tea leaves by hand, which were then dried in the sun and packed in wooden chests. The chests were loaded onto fast, sleek, sailing ships called clippers, and the tea was transported to Europe.

RAW MATERIALS

SOUTH ASIA

The Industrial Revolution in Europe led to huge demands for a wide range of raw materials from Asia, especially plant fibers grown in India, such as cotton and jute. Cotton was woven and sewn in English factories to make clothing and household textiles such as towels, sheets, and curtains. Jute was used for floor coverings and rope. In other South Asian countries, the needs of European industry led to new crops being introduced. In 1876 the first rubber trees were planted in Malaya (now Malaysia). Their sticky sap was collected and sent to Europe for use in waterproofing and to make rubber tires.

HELP FROM THE WEST

EAST ASIA

During the nineteenth century, railroads were an important sign of how forward-thinking a country was. In Japan the first railroad opened in 1872, four years after the Meiji government came to power. Japanese rulers employed foreign experts to advise them on on how to set up the latest communications systems, such as a postal service.

WORLD EXPLORATIONS

Russia ruled an enormous empire in Siberia and East Asia, and nineteenth-century Russian scientists were eager to investigate these wild and remote lands. The Russians were great sea explorers, too. In 1820, Russian navigator von Bellingshausen and two of his colleagues were probably the first people to catch sight of the vast, frozen continent of Antarctica.

WILD FRONTIERS

MIDDLE EAST

Russia ruled many lawless regions of the Middle East, which bordered the lands of the Ottoman Empire. Because Russia and the Ottomans were often at war, Russian army commanders needed to be able to transport troops and supplies safely and quickly to areas of fighting. The newly invented railroads seemed to be the answer. In the 1870s, Russian military engineers began to plan a railroad from the Middle East to Afghanistan. Locomotives were designed that would run on naphtha, a by-product of the oil refineries that were being built in large numbers in the Middle East.

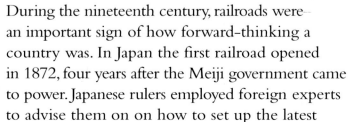

THE UNKNOWN CONTINENT

AFRICA

At the beginning of Abraham Lincoln's lifetime, people in Europe and the United States knew little about Africa, except for the Dutch and British settlements in South Africa and the ports around the coast. They did not understand African cultures and were mostly ignorant of the great civilizations that had existed in Africa in the past. During the nineteenth century, missionaries and scientists explored the African interior, making their way slowly and painfully through rain forests and across deserts, charting high mountains, great rivers, and vast lakes. By the end of the century, the spectacular scenery and wildlife of Africa were known and admired throughout the world.

LIVINGSTONE IN AFRICA

Scottish doctor and missionary David Livingstone (1813-1873) was one of the most famous European explorers. He set up a mission station in Botswana, crossed the Kalahari Desert, and explored the Zambezi River. He spent the last years of his life searching for the sources of the Congo River and the Nile River. For three years, Livingstone vanished without a trace. Journalist Henry Morton Stanley (1841–1904) went to Africa to try to find him. They met on the shores of Lake Tanganyika in 1871. Livingstone died two years later, worn out by traveling and tropical illnesses.

▼ David Livingstone spent many years exploring Africa. In this painting he has reached Lake Ngami in the Kalahari Desert.

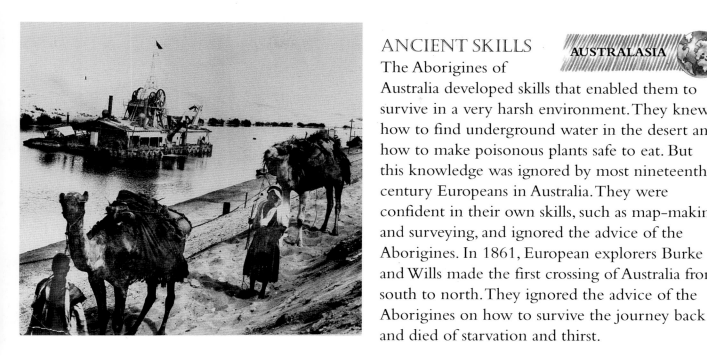

▲A dredger at work in the Suez Canal soon after it was opened. The canal needed constant dredging. This involved scooping mud from the bottom of the canal to keep its deep-water channels open for use by ocean-going ships.

THE SUEZ CANAL

In 1859, French engineer Ferdinand de Lesseps and teams of Egyptian workers began to build a new canal to join the Mediterranean with the Red Sea. It took them ten years to complete. It was named after Suez, the port where it joined the Red Sea, and was opened in 1869. The Suez Canal revolutionized travel and trade between Europe, India, Australia, and the Far East.

CONTROLLING THE CANAL

Because of the Suez Canal, ships no longer had to make the long, dangerous voyage around the southern tip of Africa. Journey times and shipping costs were reduced. The canal also made Northeast Africa very important politically. European nations wanted to control it so that they could safeguard their ships in the canal. In 1882 the British made Egypt a "protectorate," and in 1898 began to govern Sudan.

ANCIENT SKILLS

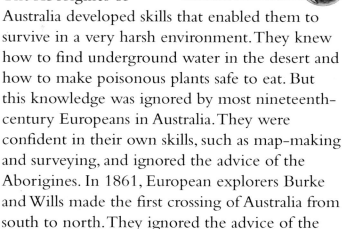
AUSTRALASIA

The Aborigines of Australia developed skills that enabled them to survive in a very harsh environment. They knew how to find underground water in the desert and how to make poisonous plants safe to eat. But this knowledge was ignored by most nineteenth-century Europeans in Australia. They were confident in their own skills, such as map-making and surveying, and ignored the advice of the Aborigines. In 1861, European explorers Burke and Wills made the first crossing of Australia from south to north. They ignored the advice of the Aborigines on how to survive the journey back and died of starvation and thirst.

▲Exhausted members of Burke and Wills' expedition close to Mount Hopeless, Australia, 1861.

FROZEN FOODS

In New Zealand one important scientific advance benefited European settlers far more than it did the native Maori people. In 1882 the first refrigerated ship reached London from New Zealand, carrying "fresh, frozen" meat and butter. Now settlers in New Zealand could sell their farm produce to a wider European market, and make more money, too.

THE CREATIVE WORLD

For thousands of years people all around the world worked with simple tools, such as brushes, chisels, looms, and potters' wheels, to create beautiful paintings, statues, fabrics, and pottery. In Africa, Asia, and parts of Eastern Europe, works of art continued to be produced using traditional techniques. But by Abraham Lincoln's time, ways of creating things were beginning to change in North America, Western Europe, and many European colonies. Men and women who enjoyed making things were now using their creative talents to design new machines, from sewing machines to harvesters. And new processes were being invented, such as photography, that relied on science to help create works of art.

▲ Drum made by the Chippewa people, who lived in the Great Lakes region of North America. It is decorated with a painting of a magical bird. Musical instruments were used in religious ceremonies and by shamans to communicate with the spirit world.

A CHANGE OF STYLE

AMERICAS

Long before the first settlers arrived in North and South America, there was a fine tradition of Native American art. Native craft workers produced beautifully decorated clothes, jewelry, pottery, rugs, and baskets for everyday use, as well as many carvings, knives, statues, bowls, and pipes. By Abraham Lincoln's day these ancient Native American traditions were in danger of being replaced by new artistic styles brought from Europe by the new settlers.

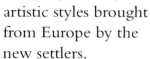

◀The arts and crafts of American settlers were often very attractive. This graceful chair was made by members of the Shaker community.

ART FOR ALL

EUROPE

During the nineteenth century new inventions changed the way art was created in many parts of Europe. Manufacturing processes developed for heavy industry were used to create art. Pottery, furniture, carpets, and even musical instruments were mass-produced in factories. For the first time, machines could produce cheap copies of an artist's work. Novels by popular writers like Charles Dickens were often published in weekly installments in magazines. Better-off people could afford to buy sheet music with tunes by leading composers, like Liszt and Beethoven.

NEW TECHNIQUES

Improved technology also created the possibility of new forms of architecture, which relied on new materials and new building techniques. Wallpapers and curtain fabrics were also available, printed with designs using new chemical dyes.

►The Crystal Palace in London, England, was a huge hall built of the new, factory-made materials, glass and cast iron. It was built to hold the Great Exhibition of 1851, which was a display of all the latest industrial machinery and mass-produced goods being made in British factories.

MAGIC CARPETS

Carpets were an ancient Middle Eastern art form, ideally suited to nomadic life. Unlike heavy, bulky, fragile furniture, they could be packed up and moved with speed and ease. Beautiful carpets, made of silk or wool or a combination of both, were produced in many Middle Eastern lands throughout the nineteenth century. Other traditional arts, especially metalwork and calligraphy (fine writing), also thrived.

►These shadow puppets are from Indonesia. The big puppet is of a wise holy man, and the small puppet is of a servant girl. They are made of painted leather on a wooden frame. Shadow puppets are still used as a popular form of storytelling in South Asia.

CLOTH AND PUPPETS

All kinds of beautiful batik cloth were created in Indonesia and nearby lands. Batik fabrics were plain pieces of material that were dyed in glowing colors to create complicated and fascinating patterns. In the same countries graceful shadow puppets were used to entertain audiences with plays based on folk tales and religious stories hundreds of years old.

WOODBLOCK PRINTS

In Japan, woodblock prints, made for sale to wealthy, well-educated collectors, were the most popular art form in the eighteenth and nineteenth centuries. The work of two great master printers, Hokusai and Hiroshige, is still admired and reprinted even today. Hokusai specialized in landscapes, such as those showing holy places like Mount Fuji or dramatic sea scenes. Hiroshige's prints are softer and gentler, and use flowers, clouds, and trees to create a tranquil, melancholy mood. (You can see one of Hiroshige's woodblock prints on page 28).

INDIAN CRAFTS

Traditional arts and crafts, such as paintings, jewelry, carvings, and statues, were created in India, too. But many Indian craft workers were also employed to produce goods especially for export to Europe, including silk and cotton fabrics patterned with European-style versions of ancient Indian designs. Indian workers constructed many fine buildings, such as the Bombay Railway Station, in an elaborate mixture of Indian and European styles.

UNCHANGED TRADITIONS

In many parts of Africa, arts and crafts continued to be made using traditional methods. In West Africa, craft workers carved wonderful statues and masks out of wood, hammered and twisted pure gold into large pieces of jewelry, and made heads and magic animal statues out of brass and bronze. Weavers and dyers created beautiful, brightly patterned textiles—some of the finest were worn only by kings and queens.

FULANI MOSQUES

Builders working for the Fulani dynasty of rulers in West Africa designed remarkable dome-shaped mosques, covered all over with a thick thatch of grass. These roofs were based on traditional house roofs and kept heavy tropical rainfall off the worshipers inside.

► Only a chief could sit here! This magnificent wooden throne was carved by craft workers in the African kingdom of Cameroon.

▲ This is a tattooed hunter from the Marquesas Islands in the Pacific, 1813. Many Pacific people believed that the gods themselves were tattooed.

THE ART OF TATTOOING

In New Zealand and the Pacific Islands, wood carvers made statues of gods and nature spirits, and decorated houses and canoes with elaborate wooden carvings in traditional swirling designs. Similar patterns were used to decorate people's bodies. Tattoos were worn by many Maori warriors as a sign of courage and pride. Stories from New Zealand explain that tattooing in a special spiral pattern was brought to earth by the legendary hero Mata-Ora after he had visited the gods.

BELIEFS AND IDEAS

In many parts of the world, the nineteenth century was a time of rapid change. New scientific discoveries made people think again about their religious and political beliefs, and there were calls for progress and reform. Sometimes, as in European countries, new ideas came from within. In other countries, such as Japan, new ideas were the result of contacts with people from elsewhere. Old and new beliefs existed side by side. But in places like North America, where settlers' ideas threatened to wipe out traditional Native Americans' beliefs, these clashes led to war.

◀This totem pole is from the Pacific coast of Canada. Totem poles were made to honor the memory of family ancestors. They also represented guardian spirits in the shape of animals and birds.

MOTHER EARTH

AMERICAS

Each Native American group had its own religious customs and ceremonies and its own myths and legends. But all groups respected the natural world and believed that the earth was their "Mother." They also believed that all living things—animals, rocks, rivers—had their own invisible spirits with the power to help or harm. Offerings of all kinds, such as gifts of food and drink and displays of dancing, were made to please these spirits.

MISSIONARIES

The earliest European settlers in the Americas were mostly Christians. They built churches and schools and sent missionaries to North and South America to try to convert Native Americans. These missionaries did not always succeed. For example, in parts of South America and the Caribbean, their Christian teaching became mixed with traditional beliefs to create a new faith.

BLESSED BY GOD

Many European settlers believed that Native American civilization was primitive. They thought that European religious beliefs were superior and had been blessed by God. They believed that the European lifestyle was destined to replace Native American ways.

NEW RELIGIONS

Many new religious ideas grew in the United States. A preacher called Joseph Smith believed he had been sent special messages from God. He led his people westward. After Smith was murdered, Brigham Young led the group. In 1847 they set up a community in Salt Lake City, Utah, based on the teachings of Smith's new Mormon religion.

In 1774 a group of Shakers settled in New York State. Their community grew during the nineteenth century. The Shakers lived simply, making their own furniture and growing their own food. They did not marry, but led a single life, and refused to go to war.

►The Shakers originated in England. They migrated to the United States looking for religious freedom. Their religious worship included trembling, dancing, and falling into trances.

THE RIGHT TO BE FREE

Slavery was a controversial issue in Europe as well as in the United States. Antislavery activists, led by British statesman William Wilberforce, campaigned for 20 years before the slave trade was banned in 1807. Slavery itself was not made illegal in Great Britain until 1833. Wilberforce was supported during his campaign by his deeply held Christian beliefs. He and his followers were nicknamed "the Saints." France and Spain followed Britain's example and banned their ships from slave trading in 1818 and 1820.

▼ This nineteenth-century picture of an African slave was made to celebrate Wilberforce's success in getting the slave trade banned. The slave in the picture is about to be freed.

▲ Eleven peaceful protesters were killed by soldiers in the Peterloo Massacre, which took place in St. Peter's Fields, Manchester, England.

THE RIGHT TO VOTE

In England, protesters demanded that Parliament should be reformed so it could better represent the views and needs of ordinary people. They also wanted working men to be given the right to vote. These demands increased after an incident in Manchester in 1819, known as the Peterloo Massacre. Soldiers fired into a crowd of peaceful protesters who were demanding parliamentary reform. Eleven people were killed. Eventually, in 1832 and 1867, Parliament passed laws to increase the number of people who were allowed to vote. But this right was not given to all adult men until 1918. Women had to wait until 1928 before they could vote on the same terms as men.

REVOLUTIONARY IDEAS

In mainland Europe there were also demands for government reform. In 1848, the Year of Revolutions, there were riots in many European cities. In the same year, Karl Marx, a German writer living in London, published a book called the *Communist Manifesto*. In it he demanded greater freedom and better pay for ordinary people. He urged: "Workers of the world, unite! You have nothing to lose but your chains!"

HUMAN ORIGINS

New scientific ideas excited many people in nineteenth-century Europe. They were fascinated by the discoveries made by naturalist Charles Darwin on his expedition to study wildlife around the world from 1831 to 1836. A few years later they were shocked when Darwin published his ideas on how humans evolved. He argued that humans developed from earlier primitive ancestors.

REFORMS

MIDDLE EAST

Over the centuries, Muslim communities in the Middle East had developed different ways of worshiping Allah (God). These included singing, dancing, and visiting the tombs of saints and Sufis. But by Lincoln's time a group of religious reformers called Wahhabis (named after their founder Muhammad ibn Abd al-Wahhab) believed these were wrong. They wanted simpler ways of worship and a return to laws based on the Muslim holy book, the Qur'an. Wahhabi ideas inspired Sheik Muhammad ibn Saud to unite almost all the lands of Arabia into a single kingdom, ruled by Muslim laws.

THE DIVINE SOCIETY

SOUTH ASIA

In India, religious beliefs and political ideas were mingled together. Most Indian people followed the Hindu faith, although there were many Buddhists, Muslims, Sikhs, and Parsees. In 1828 a Hindu religious reformer, Rajah Ram Mohan Roy, founded the Spiritual Society. This was a religious movement that aimed to ban ancient rituals from Hindu religious ceremonies. For example, he banned idol worship and suttee—the custom that forced a wife to commit suicide when her husband died. He also campaigned for Indians to have the right to govern their own land.

►Kali was the Indian goddess of bloodshed and death. Her followers believed that it was their duty to sacrifice people as offerings to her.

INVISIBLE SPIRITS

Most people in East Asia
followed three ancient traditional religions—
Confucianism, Daoism, and Buddhism.
But some people, especially in Mongolia,
Korea, and Japan, also worshiped
invisible spirits. They believed these
spirits lived in mountains, rivers, and
trees. Special priests called shamans
believed they could enter the spirit world
by ritual chanting, drumming, and dancing
and sometimes by taking drugs. Shamans
worked to help the community. They tried
to find good hunting grounds, control the
weather, drive away bad luck, and heal the sick.

◀This shaman
from northeastern
Asia is dressed
in magnificent
robes decorated
with amulets
and charms.
He is carrying
a drum to call up
the spirits and a
stick with little
jingling bells.

GODS, KINGS, AND PRIESTS

In Africa, religious ideas varied from nation
to nation. But most African people believed
in a god (or several gods) who protected their
homeland, gave them children, made the rains
fall, and helped their crops and livestock to grow.
Sometimes the gods spoke through kings or
priests, and sometimes they were represented by
carved statues or masks. African people also
believed in powerful spirits that could bring
good luck or disease and disaster. They believed
that the spirits of dead ancestors could help
them if they were treated with respect. So
families made offerings to ancestors' spirits
at special shrines, where the bones of dead
ancestors were kept in beautifully decorated
containers carved from wood.

◀Masks were worn in many different
African religious ceremonies. They
might represent dead ancestors or holy
spirits. Some masks were believed to
have special powers of their own.

MISSIONARIES

After around 1860 many Christian missionaries from Europe arrived in Africa and began to teach their own faith. They felt it was their duty to lead other people to become Christians. Many missionaries gave their lives to this cause. Some died from tropical diseases, and some were murdered by African leaders who feared the missionaries' teaching would destroy their people's ancient way of life.

HOLY PEOPLE

AUSTRALASIA

In Australia and New Zealand, gods, spirits, and dead people, such as family ancestors, were honored in special ceremonies with singing and dancing. Sometimes people taking part in personal ceremonies, such as one to mark the change from childhood to adulthood, were treated as if they were holy. In New Zealand being tattooed was a sign of reaching adulthood. During a tattooing ceremony, food was not allowed to touch the tattooed person's lips, so it was poured down the throat through a special wooden funnel.

GHOSTS AND DEMONS

The peoples of the Pacific Islands worshiped many different gods. Each god or goddess had special powers—creating dry land, controlling animals and plants, sending good harvests, causing earthquakes, or bringing rain. These gods and goddesses might appear in all kinds of terrifying shapes and forms, such as erupting volcanoes, sea monsters, or ghosts. Pacific Islanders also feared the spirits of the dead, which haunted burial grounds. They thought that some spirits were seeking a final resting place beyond the sea and the sky. They thought others were looking for new spirit bodies, which they would enter and take over in order to be reborn as dangerous demons.

▼Aborigine dancers taking part in a religious ceremony called a corroboree in Tasmania in 1830. They painted their bodies to look like spirits from the Dreamtime, a magical age long ago when ancestors and spirits created the world. The ceremony takes place at night.

PEOPLES FROM AROUND THE WORLD

Aborigines The first inhabitants of Australia, who arrived there about 40,000 years ago.

Ashante The people who lived in present-day Ghana, Togo, and the Ivory Coast. Also the name of an independent kingdom in the same region of Africa during the 1700s and 1800s.

Chinook People who lived on the northwestern coast of the United States. They caught fish and carved huge totem poles.

Chippewa People who lived in the Great Lakes region of North America. They were hunters and farmers.

Dinka Seminomadic cattle-herding people who lived in the Upper Nile Valley, part of present-day Sudan.

Fulani A group of Muslim cattle-herding peoples who set up a powerful West African kingdom in the early 1800s.

Hidatsa People who lived in the Missouri River valley in present-day North Dakota. They built earth lodges, raised corn, and hunted buffalo.

Inuit Native Americans who arrived in the Arctic regions of North America about 2000 B.C.

Mandan People who lived in the Missouri River valley, in present-day North Dakota,. They built earth lodges, raised corn, and hunted buffalo.

Maori Settlers in New Zealand who came from the Pacific islands from about A.D. 800.

Masai Hunters and cattle-herders who lived on the savannas (dry grasslands) of East Africa in present-day Kenya and nearby.

Mtetwa The people who controlled southern Africa before the Zulus became powerful.

Native Americans The first inhabitants of the Americas, who arrived there about 30,000 years ago. Native Americans were divided into more than 200 different groups, with different lifestyles and languages.

Native peoples The original inhabitants of any country or the people who have been born and brought up there.

Paiute Nomadic people who lived in the dry Great Basin region of North America. They survived by gathering wild foods.

Zulus A group of peoples who lived in southern Africa. In the early 1800s, led by Shaka, they joined together and conquered a large empire. Zulu power collapsed in 1879 after Zulu warriors were defeated by European settlers.

amulets Lucky charms.

archaeology The study of the past from remains such as bones, coins, pottery, and the ruins of old buildings.

assassinated Killed by political enemies.

batik A type of cloth, produced in Indonesia and nearby lands. It is decorated by painting patterns on the cloth with wax, and then dying it, using brilliant colors. The area painted with wax does not absorb the dye. The wax is removed from the cloth, leaving elaborate designs made up of dyed and undyed areas of fabric.

blight A disease (usually of plants) that causes them to wither and rot.

Buddhism A religion based on the teachings of prince Siddhartha Gautama, who lived in India in the sixth century B.C. He taught his followers to seek truth and the right way to live through meditation (quiet thinking).

Christian A person who believes in and follows the teachings of Jesus Christ.

civil rights The right of ordinary people to play a full part in society, including the right to vote, receive an education, have a job, marry and have children, and follow their own religious faith.

civil war War between different groups of people within one country.

colonial Belonging to a colony— a country or region that is is ruled by a stronger, foreign power.

commons Open spaces of countryside where villagers had rights to feed animals and gather firewood.

Confucianism A way of living based on the teachings of Confucius, who lived in China about 551–479 B.C. He believed in family loyalty, right behavior, and treating people justly.

Congress Part of the U.S. government. Members of Congress debate government policies, vote to collect taxes, and make new laws.

Daoism A way of living based on the belief that returning to nature is the right way to live.

democratic Used to describe a system of government in which ordinary citizens have a right to choose their leaders and to comment freely on government policies.

drainage A system of ditches and underground pipes installed so that surplus water can flow away.

emancipation Often used to mean "freedom from slavery."

French Revolution The period 1789–1799 when the people of France rebelled against the French king and queen and executed them along with thousands of nobles and priests. They then introduced a new form of government based on the principles of "Liberty" (freedom) and "Equality." The Revolution collapsed after revolutionary leaders argued among themselves and because many French people became sickened by the fighting and bloodshed.

frontier A boundary between different nations; land next to an undeveloped region.

government policies What a government plans and does.

gun foundries Special factories and workshops where metal guns were made.

HMS His (or Her) Majesty's Ship —part of the the name given to all warships in the British Navy.

humid Damp or moist.

improved cattle Cattle that grew bigger and stronger and produced more meat.

manuring schemes The scientific spreading of manure (animal dung) on farmland to improve it. Manure added important chemicals to the soil and made crops grow better.

mosques Buildings in which Muslims gather to say prayers and listen to readings from the Muslim holy book, the Qur'an.

naturalist Someone who studies wild animals and plants.

Ottoman Empire The lands ruled by members of the Ottoman dynasty (ruling family) in eastern Europe, North Africa, and the Middle East. The Ottoman capital city was Istanbul, Turkey.

paddy fields Flooded fields where rice is grown.

panning for gold Searching for gold by sieving the fine silt at the bottom of rivers in the hope of finding tiny fragments of gold.

people A group that lives together as one nation or that is united under one government or by religious faith or origins.

plantains Fruit related to bananas, usually picked while green and cooked before eating.

proclamation An official announcement.

protectorate A country that has been taken over by a stronger country that offers to protect it.

Republican Party A political party in the U.S., founded in 1854 to fight against the extension of slavery.

sabers Long, curved swords.

savanna Dry, rolling grasslands.

sawmill A factory in which tree-trunks are sawed into boards.

sorghum A grasslike plant that produces edible seeds, which can be ground to make flour, or syrup from the stalks.

state governments The elected rulers who governed all the separate states in the U.S.

Sufis Muslim mystics—people who devoted their lives to prayer and meditation (quiet thinking) about God.

surveyor Someone whose job it is to measure land and determine boundaries.

typhoon A violent tropical storm, from the Chinese words for "great wind."

yam A tropical plant that produces edible roots.

zoology The study of animals.

INDEX